T0114787

Expressions from the Heart and Spirit

A Collection of Poems and Songs

MARY STANCIL

WESTBOW
PRESS®
A DIVISION OF THOMAS NELSON
& ZONDERVAN

WestBow Press books may be ordered through booksellers or by contacting:

WestBow Press
A Division of Thomas Nelson & Zondervan
1663 Liberty Drive
Bloomington, IN 47403
www.westbowpress.com
844-714-3454

Scripture quotations marked KJV are from the Holy Bible, King James Version (Authorized Version). First published in 1611. Quoted from the KJV Classic Reference Bible, Copyright © 1983 by The Zondervan Corporation.

ISBN: 979-8-3850-0372-3 (sc)
ISBN: 979-8-3850-0376-1 (hc)
ISBN: 979-8-3850-0377-8 (e)

Library of Congress Control Number: 2023921681

Print information available on the last page.

WestBow Press rev. date: 11/15/2023

DEDICATION

This book is dedicated to Jesus Christ, my Lord and Savior.

> The Lord hath called me from the womb, from the bowels of my mother hath he made mention of my name.
>
> And he hath made my mouth like a sharp sword: in the shadow of his hand he hid me, and made me a polished shaft, in his quiver hath he hid me,"
>
> And said unto me, Thou art my servant, O Israel, in whom I will be glorified.
>
> —Isaiah 49:1b-3

CONTENTS

INTRODUCTION

Over the years, a pencil and paper have been two of my dearest friends. When I could get no one to listen to me or answer any of my questions, I would grab my paper and pencil and communicate through the written word.

Since very early in my life, I've had a close relationship with God. Yet there have been many times when I found myself in the pit of depression. It would be many years before I realized why.

But whatever my mood, the Lord spoke to me. Many times He spoke through His Word, the Holy Bible, and at times, through words given to me, which I wrote down on paper.

This book is a selection of some of those writings. I hope you can identify with the feelings put forth through these words. And I pray that you will be uplifted and encouraged to see what God can do for us if we only ask and believe.

May God bless you as you read, and may He use it to glorify Himself.

CHAPTER 1

Despair

The sorrows of death compassed me, and the floods of ungodly men made me afraid.

The sorrows of hell compassed me about: the snares of death prevented me.

—Psalm 18:4–5 KJV

Despair

Today I feel full of woe.
I feel I have no place to go.
No one to turn to who'll understand.
Nowhere I find a helping hand.

I feel I have no reason to live.
I feel I have nothing to give.
The world is like a lonely cell;
I feel as though I'm in a jail.

I look for something to set me free.
No hope for the future do I see.
Nothing makes a difference to me.
The misery I have is just *to be*.

To be alive is pain and sorrow.
I wouldn't care if I saw tomorrow.
The flowers no longer bloom for me.
The beauties of earth, no longer I see.

If I could die and cause no pain,
If my death were not in vain,
I'd die today! I'd die right now.
"But, oh Lord, I don't know how."

I don't know how to live or die.
I don't know the reason for anything. Why?
Why live? Or why die? Oh!
Where does the answer lie?

I must find it, the reason to live.
Otherwise, I have nothing to give.
No joy, no happiness, no peace.
Somehow I must find release!

Somehow, I have to free my soul.
That will be my only goal.
"Oh Lord, help me learn to live.
Don't let me die with nothing to give."

Tired of Living

I'm so tired of living.
I wish today were my last day.
It seems I'm always giving,
While nothing comes my way.

It seems that no one's ever cared
What really happened to me.
And when the truth is finally shared,
I'll be right; you'll see.

It seems somehow I've always failed
At all I've tried to do.
As a mother (failed), as a wife (failed).
As a woman, I've failed too.

It seems I've lived a hundred years
Instead of just twenty-two.
Most in sadness and in tears,
And sometimes a smile or two.

The tears somehow outnumber the smiles.
The sadness outweighs the joy.
I'm tired as though I'd run for miles.
I have as much life as a toy.

That's why I'm tired of living here
And doing the things I do.
And I really find reason to cheer
When I hope it will soon be through.

Death seems like a refreshing sleep.
A sleep I would like to know,
A sleep that will slowly creep.
Much better than life, I know.

After Death

Don't put on dresses and suits of black.
Don't wish for a moment that I was back.
I never was happy all the while.
But now, with my Jesus, I can smile.

He took away the scars of the dead.
He wiped away the tears I had shed.
He told me He loved me and died for me.
And finally, at last, I could see.

Don't mourn for me, and please don't cry.
You don't understand: I *had* to die.
I had to flee from this world and its pain.
I had to be happy again.

At last, He made me happy and free.
So please, don't feel sorry for me.
I loved Him so much; my love was so great.
I had to die; I couldn't wait.

July 5, 1971

A year ago today,
Someone I loved passed away.
I can't explain the way I felt
As before the throne of God I knelt.

As I knelt, I asked Him, "Why?"
I prayed that I, too, would die.
I felt as though my heart would break.
I never before felt such an ache.

No more sorrow, no more tears.
No more pain, no more fears.
A person with a smile for everyone,
At last, her task on earth was done.

The days of a year have flickered by.
I no longer ask the reason why.
We all must laugh, we all must cry,
We all must live, we all must die.

Yesterday

Day after day, I find
I still can't get him off my mind.
The one who meant so much to me,
In my mind and dreams I see.

It's been months since I've seen his face,
But I remember every single trace.
His dark hair and eyes, his gentle touch,
His loving smile I miss so much.

If I could only turn back the days
To a time before we went our separate ways.
If I could just relive one day,
I'm sure I would do it another way.

But I can't recapture the past,
Those wonderful days that passed too fast.
I'll have to go on my way
And try to forget yesterday.

For Love of Him

Into my life there came a man.
I knew but did not understand.
It wasn't long before I could see
That close to him, I wanted to be.

As I look back through my mind,
Hours of stolen love unwind.
And for a moment, my heartbeat races,
Remembering his warm kisses and gentle embraces.

The love I felt for him was so strong,
I forgot the differences between right and wrong.
All the things we did and shared
Convinced me that he really cared.

I found I loved him more than life.
I found I wanted to become his wife.
I wanted us always to be
This close for all eternity.

I guess I knew—just like in the past—
The beautiful, happy time wouldn't last.
The things that we did together
Will live in my heart forever and ever.

We've lost each other now, it seems.
We're only together in my dreams.
But one lasting bond there'll always be,
The love I feel inside of me.

Out of my life there walked a man
I loved but could not understand.
He only let me close enough to find I love him;
He's always on my mind.

Who Do You See?

As I look around,
It's pitiful to see
All the people who laugh
Just to hide their misery.

They try to please others.
To be what others want them to be.
So the person who is seen
Is who they want others to see.

I guess we're all a little like that.
We're all a little bit fake.
But if we would learn to be ourselves,
We would be spared a lot of heartache.

Sometimes we carry the whole thing
Just a little too far.
While trying to please others,
We forget who we really are.

That's why it's so important
To be ourselves all the time.
Then life becomes so much easier,
And we live with peace of mind.

What Is a Friend?
Are There Any Real Friends?

For the first time in my life,
I thought I had a friend.
Someone who would love me at all times,
Stick with me to the end.

But then when the real me showed through,
All my "friends" were gone.
And now, at a time when I need the most help,
I find myself all alone.

I've always tried to be a true friend
To all those around me.
But they've forgotten all the good in my life,
And only the bad they see.

I've reached out to them,
Begged them to be my friends,
Only to be hurt over and over,
Rejected again and again.

I look to the future.
No hope do I see.
I can't continue to put on a face,
And I can't afford to be me.

They've got it all made up in their minds.
They pity and look down on me.
Could it be that in my mistakes,
Their own they clearly see?

I don't know that I can go on
With all the falseness around.
Those who say one thing and do another,
Put on a smile where there's really a frown.

They've condemned me for the way I am,
Not trying to understand.
They only push me further away
As I desperately reach for their hand.

How am I to pick up and go on
With nothing to go on to?
No one there to help me along
When I don't know what to do.

Maybe if I search long enough,
I'll find a Christian who's what he should be,
Who really loves God with his whole heart.
And because of that, can love *even me*.

Alone and Lonely

I'm one of the lonely people
You see each Sunday at church.
I sit beneath the steeple,
A smile concealing my hurts.

I've tried so hard to be a part
Of this body who claim to love.
But somehow, I just never fit it.
To speak to me, they're above.

Do you know what it's like
To be in a crowd and yet be alone?
The sad part is that I'm still alone
Even when I go home.

I'm reaching out to someone,
But there is nobody there.
I long to have somebody love me,
But nobody gives me a care.

I've reached the end of my rope.
Time is running out.
I've given up trying to hope.
All I want now is a way out.

The sad part is no one will know I'm gone.
No one will miss me at all.
Life will go on the same as usual.
Without me, it should be a ball.

If you are one of the lonely people,
I know just how you feel.
I pray you will find someone who cares
Before you, too, lie cold and still.

Where Is Love?
All I Wanted Was Love

With my heart in many pieces,
I awake each morning and pray.
And I ask the Lord of mercy
To please let this be my last day.

As I walk, weary and weak and alone
Down life's fast-paced, hurried road,
No one will take time to listen to me
As I'm crushed under life's heavy load.

I guess no one can see or hear me
As I lie trapped beneath the ground.
They are so busy with their own lives,
They haven't noticed I'm no longer around.

Don't they care about my torment
As I lie trapped within this grave?
If someone doesn't come real soon,
There will be nothing left of me to save.

For I've lost so many pieces of my heart—
Given freely because I care—
That soon, my heart will cease to beat
Because, in a coffin, there is no air.

And there are so few pieces of my heart left,
I'm not even sure I could survive.
I feel like I'm already dead,
And there's just an empty shell, barely alive.

The cold winds of winter are always with me.
I have nothing left; I've lost everything.
I wait and yearn desperately, but only a flicker of hope remains
That I will ever survive the winter to see the spring.

And as the tears roll down my cheek again,
As they so often do every day,
I ask myself, "What difference does it make?
It doesn't matter anyway."

My life has been one long, lonely road
As I desperately cried out to be loved.
At last I realize there is no love here,
Only people who use you; then out the door you're shoved.

On second thought, this place is not that bad.
Soon I'll escape all the hurt and the pain.
I'll never be convinced to open up and allow
Myself to be rejected or abused ever again.

It's only through death that I will find love.
There is none to be found here, not even a friend.
I'm tired of fighting a losing battle.
My question finally answered, at last, my hurt will end.

Regrets and More Questions

If I could but turn back the clock
To a time which has already passed,
I would gently embrace every moment,
And live and enjoy them while they last.

I would look at time differently,
Not assuming that I always had more.
Realizing that nothing lasts forever,
That constant change is what's in store.

If we could but have the knowledge
About life and what's important when we're born,
There would be a lot less pain,
And fewer hearts and lives torn.

What is the purpose of this journey
That starts without our choice or will?
And we race down its road frantically
Until our heart and soul we kill.

What is this hectic thing called life
That we find ourselves captive in?
And when we make all the moves,
Does anybody ever win?

We rarely find the things we seek.
We settle for less but yearn for more.
And if our dream should come along,
It is too late to pursue it for sure.

It takes all our energy
Just to live from day to day.
And life is just a big circle
That we start and end the same way.

Questioning Life

As I awoke this morning
And saw the sunshine and blue sky,
I didn't want to get out of bed.
The constant question still in my head, *Why?*

All my energy has vanished,
Along with the dark of the night.
And I'm more tired now than
When I laid down in bed.
Gone are the days of my get up and go,
And I have no desire to fight.

The world is all different now.
I don't know truth from a lie.
I don't know a friend from an enemy.
So I grope in the darkness and cry.

Who decides which paths we take?
Is the decision really ours to make?
Can we change anything that's been planned?
Or are the things that happen just something
We have to take?

Are some chosen to receive only good
And some to receive only bad?
Or is there some of both, chosen for all of us?
Sometimes we laugh; sometimes we're sad.

Are there some chosen to be with others
And some chosen to live alone?
Who makes the decision? Or how are we picked?
In the end, will the answers all be known?

If This is Life

Oh, if I could but escape
The bars that imprison me.
If I could but break the chains
That immobilize and will not set me free.

Their hold on me gets tighter day by day.
They drain the hope from deep within my soul.
There is no future to look forward to.
Fleeing from my prison is my goal.

I lie upon my bed engulfed in doom.
A never-ending sorrow blankets me.
I dream of falling into a sleep and ne'er awake.
The only way I see to be set free.

Torment and pain my constant companions.
Any friends I had have now abandoned me.
I talk out loud to hear another voice,
The loneliness and misery attempting to flee.

Oh, if someone could hear my cry for help
And care enough to listen to what I dare not speak,
And find some compassion for my present state
And help to hold me up while I'm so weak.

To believe that could happen
Is just a fantasy.
And reality reminds me again
That I blew any chance that could ever be.

I'm destined to remain against my will—
Alone, abandoned, and unloved.
I pray without ceasing to be set free.
But no answer do I receive from above.

I wonder what I've done to be so marked?
But then I know you don't have to do some terrible wrong.
You can give and love and help others and neglect yourself,
And feel nothing in return, no matter how much you long.

Oh, death, I request that you take me away,
Leaving the bars and chains behind.
My spirit released to fly free
And erase all the pain from my mind

Too Little, Too Late

My family all gather around me
Now that I'm no longer here.
They stand around and mourn.
But in life, it was abundantly clear.

When they were young and needed me,
I cooked and cleaned and read and played
And listened when they needed to talk.
I devoted my life to God and them,
Showing them the right path to walk.

They couldn't talk or spend enough time with me
When I worked and made plenty of money.
I bought them lots of things we could never afford.
I was strong and in charge, and Jim still called me "honey."

Then my mind opened, and all
This garbage started pouring out.
It took its toll on my body and mind.
My sanity became a definite doubt.

God led me to a doctor who listened
To what I said and cared enough to hear.
We started to work with prayer and guidance.
But the outcome was still unclear.

He gave unselfishly of his time and encouragement.
For the first time, I experienced a friend's love.
No other person on earth had ever helped me this way.
I learned that love not only came from above.

Surrounded by the love of the staff at the clinic,
I started to move forward.
The things I remembered seemed easier to bear
As, with love, my recovery we moved toward.

I became convinced that I could overcome
All that my memory threw toward me.
With the help of God and my newfound friends,
I was sure that someday I'd be free.

My future started to look bright.
I looked forward to each new day.
With a lot of hard work and support from my friends,
My recovery was well on its way.

But just as the dawn was the brightest,
I was dealt a deadly blow:
They told me it was time to try it on my own.
Though I fought to stay, they made me go.

So I left all alone, not knowing where to begin.
My listener was gone; my friends were gone too.
With no support system and no one to listen,
Where was I to go and what was I to do?

My family did not know how to deal
With the illness that had taken over my world.
I could no longer work or function like a "supermom."
There was no one to lean on, so the thoughts in my mind swirled.

Feeling that everything had been taken from me,
I despaired, trying to figure out, Why?
What had I done to cause them to send me away?
This was not life, so why not just die?

Convinced that no one would miss me—
They all wanted me to go away—
I opened a bottle of pills and swallowed them all.
That I could go to sleep and ne'er wake, I prayed.

But God would not let me die.
And I faced the hatred of family and friends.
My state was much worse now than before
As I watched helplessly, all my relationships end.

It's said that time will heal all things.
Don't believe them; it isn't true.
It's been five years, and I'm still dead inside.
My body is left in torment; I pray it soon will die too.

I still have no one to listen.
But it really doesn't matter anymore.
My whole family thinks I am out of my mind.
So what would they come and see me for?

They don't believe that I'm physically sick,
So they're not here when I need them.
Some don't even call to ask about me
'Cause they really don't care how I am.

They don't come around because I can't do for them.
My grandchildren won't even know me.
They'll tell them that I've gone to live with Jesus.
And after a few days, there'll be nothing left to see.

So they come now to lay me to rest.
They had no time to give me when I was alone.
They'll do what's expected, and put me in the ground.
And what will show I was ever here—a cold stone.

Will You Miss Me?

Will you miss me when I'm gone?
Or will it seem as though I was never here?
Will you think of what we shared
And laugh or maybe shed a tear?

I know that life is busy,
With its fast-paced go, go, go.
And we all have more than we can do.
But don't let the important things go.

A job, money, and what these can buy,
Things that make it easier for you to live.
But when compared to family and spiritual things,
Which has the most to give?

As we live our lives in a hurry,
We must make time to spend
With those who brought us into the world
Before their time in this world comes to an end.

You don't want to stand at a grave site,
Wishing that they were still here.
Wishing you had spent more time with them.
The truth was never more clear.

How much time does it take to dial a number,
To talk for a minute or two,
To find out how they are and if they need anything?
Is there anything for them you need to do?

A few minutes a day can save the heartache
Of wishing you had done more.
The peace of mind it can give
When they cross over to the other shore.

If you take a few minutes now
To make how you feel clear,
We won't have to sit and wonder
If you'll miss us when we're not here.

CHAPTER 2

Cry for Help

In my distress I called upon the Lord, and cried unto my God. He heard my voice out of His temple, and my cry came before Him, even into His ears.

—Psalm 18:6

Truth

A reflection in the mirror I see.
Why does it not look like me?
A stranger is what I see.
Where is the person I used to be?

A young girl gentle, loving, and true.
Oh, when did she turn into you,
A person full of evil and hate?
Was this a trick played by fate?

My true self I finally see.
Where will the truth lead me?
A better person day by day?
"Oh, Lord, is this the right way?"

With all my faults I'll cope.
And this will be my only hope.
Someday I'll look again and see
That the reflection in the mirror is *me*.

Souvenirs and the Wilderness

What is a souvenir?
A memory from the past,
Something that remains in your heart
To make a special time last.

It can also be a material thing,
Something you can see with the eye.
Little things we pull out from time to time
To remember times that have gone by.

What is the wilderness?
Anyplace that's away from God.
Anywhere we are when we're not
On the narrow path we're to trod.

It can be in the midst of others,
And yet, we can feel all alone.
Even with loved ones around,
We feel far away from home.

You may ask, "What in the world
Are you trying to say?
What do souvenirs and the wilderness
Have in common anyway?"

We can't depend on souvenirs.
They sometimes get in the way.
Sometimes we long to live in the past
And forget about living today.

We only go to the wilderness
To go through a time of learning.
But after a time of quiet listening,
For our homeland we start yearning.

Souvenirs and the wilderness
Should not be a way of living.
There is too much love locked up inside;
Love to others we should be giving.

"Oh, Lord, I pray You will use me,
And take away all my fears.
Don't let me stay in the wilderness,
Crying over my souvenirs."

Where Is My Joy?

Where is the joy that once was mine?
Joy not experienced for a very long time.
The peaceful feeling deep inside,
That here, my Lord would always abide?

Has my Lord forsaken me?
Has my Lord forgotten me?
Certainly not! He is always there
If I just turn to Him in prayer.

How long have I been out of His Word?
How long since His voice I heard?
How long since I knelt in prayer
And bared my soul before Him there?

Surely ten years hasn't passed
Since I felt His joy last?
But the calendar confirms my fears.
"Oh God, I've wasted ten precious years.

"My God, I ask that You forgive me
For the wasteful way I've learned to live.
Restore to me the joy I've lost.
I'm finally willing to pay the cost.

"Fill me with Your Spirit again.
Give me love, peace, and joy within.
Make Your presence evident to others,
So I can minister to my sisters and brothers.

"Oh Lord, make up for the years,
I spent hiding in fear and doubt.
Oh Lord, open my eyes to see,
And lead me to true victory.

"Lord, as I stand quiet and still,
Place me in the center of Your will.
Restore Your joy within my heart,
And never again will I depart."

Lord, Let Me See through Your Eyes

As I look at the world around me,
I don't understand what I see.
And I ask my Father the question,
"How can You allow this to be?"

Wickedness and evil everywhere,
Abounding on every hand.
And as I look at our nation,
I wonder how long it can stand.

It seems everything is backwards;
Nothing is the way it should be.
So I ask Him to open my eyes
And allow me through His eyes to see.

But as He begins to open my eyes,
It seems my view has changed.
All my feelings and questions,
It seems, have been rearranged.

I realize that as He looks at the world,
He doesn't see at all what I see.
He sees the world through eyes of love,
The love that sent Him to die for you and me.

He sees people not for what they are
But what, with His help, they can be.
And as I realize this, I'm so thankful
That this is also the way He sees me.

"Oh Lord, forgive me for judging others
Of things that I'm guilty of too.
And fill my heart so full of Your love,
I'll do what You've called me to do.

"Help me not to sit back and condemn
But get busy, for there's plenty to do.
And love You and serve You with all my heart,
And leave all the rest up to You."

Feelings

Where are the feelings that once were mine,
Feelings not experienced for a very long time?
Laughter, joy, peace, and love deep inside
That I believed would always abide.

Even sadness, hurt, pain, and fears
Have been hidden away for many years.
Try as you may, you can still handle only so much
Before with your real feelings, you start to lose touch.

As life becomes worse and days pass by,
It becomes harder for someone to make you cry.
You harden yourself so when things you can't bear
Begin to start happening, you pretend you're not there.

After a while, you learn to stand back and see
The awful things happening to the person named *me*.
But you don't try to stop it because you believe
That you deserve the terrible treatment you receive.

You've been told all your life how bad you are,
How you'll never accomplish anything or go far.
That even if you do something good and should be glad,
There are no feelings there, not glad, not sad.

The door is opening slowly, and feelings are coming out.
Am I happy? Am I scared? Do I want to cry or shout?
I'm not sure what I'm feeling as my body comes alive.
But my main goal, to become whole, is why I strive.

Before me lies a mountain to climb
That I can only take a day at a time.
With the Lord Jesus as my guide and friend,
Safely at the top, my journey will end.

In order to retain the good, I must relive the bad.
But when it's all finished, I know I'll be glad.
I'm so tired of not feeling anything, being numb.
Sometimes I wish, like a flood, they would all come.

May I continue to praise the Lord even in pain
Because it's only through it that I can feel joy again.
Real joy that floods the soul and brings peace within,
So you feel the love of God as if you never sinned.

"Lord, help me learn to feel
So that through me, others You might heal.
Lord, I ask that You make me whole,
So I can serve You with all my heart and soul.

"Lord, open my mind to remember the past.
Help me to know the answers at last.
Why did those things happen to me?
Show me the truth, and I shall be free!"

CHAPTER 3

Deliverance

He sent from above, He took me, He drew me out of many waters. He delivered me from my strong enemy, and from them which hated me: for they were too strong for me. They prevented me in the day of my calamity: but the Lord was my stay. He brought me forth also into a large place; He delivered me, because He delighted in me.

—Psalm 18:16–19

Finding Deliverance

Today my Savior called to me.
My first reaction was to flee.
To run as far away as I could
To forget about the just and the good.

My Savior again I found today.
Somehow I had wandered far away.
It saddened His heart and made Him cry
To know how much I wanted to die.

He wanted me on this earth to stay.
My purpose: To show others the way.
To tell them He loves them one and all,
The very big and the very small.

My life had been short, my works too few.
He understood I was sad and blue.
He wanted my soul to be filled with joy
That He had saved me forevermore.

He told me joy in His work I must find
If I ever wanted to free my mind.
The mind I felt was ready to break,
The mind He was not ready to take.

He told me not to worry or fret,
That through Him, I could forget
The problems and troubles that chained my mind,
The sickness that had made me blind.

I could no longer see my God;
Nor find the narrow path He trod.
I could not see my fellow man.
Nothing could I understand.

I'm glad my Jesus wouldn't let me flee.
I'm glad that He held onto me.
I'm glad He took me by the hand.
I'm glad He made me understand.

I'm glad my Jesus came that way.
I'm glad He loved me and died one day
To save the souls of all who received.
At last, I feel my burden relieved.

Who Me—Lost?

With my life in a million pieces,
Confused and empty inside,
I began to realize that I was lost.
Desperately, I searched for a place to hide.

How could I possibly be lost?
I'd been a church member for many years.
All of the things I had done in the church,
Now it filled me with overwhelming fears.

How could I face the people?
What would they say or do?
What would they think of me
If I allowed the real me to show through?

All these thoughts flooded my mind.
I could not eat or sleep.
All the pressure building within,
How much longer could it keep?

I had to talk to someone,
So to my pastor I went.
And as I unraveled the horrible facts,
I knew to this place I'd been sent.

I could not leave that night
Until a decision I'd reached.
Too many times I sat and heard God's Word
And saw Jesus as this man preached.

I knelt there in his study
And asked Jesus to enter my heart.
I had no idea what lay in store
As on my new life I did start.

I turned my life over to Jesus,
Thinking He would fix my mess.
But instead, He turned my life upside down
And started to remove my sinfulness.

I didn't like the things He did.
Over my life I had no say.
Nothing turned out the way I planned.
In the Potter's hands, my life was now clay.

I tried to take back the things I said.
I tried to undo what I had done.
But I didn't realize I no longer belonged to myself.
Now I belonged to the Son.

I refused to look up and listen.
I didn't want to hear what He said.
And so as my stubbornness persisted,
I ended up, on my back, in bed.

I hid my face in a book,
Trying to occupy my mind.
Trying to keep from listening.
Trying to pretend I was blind.

Then I got so sick
I couldn't hold up a book.
The only thing I had strength to do
Was listen as upward I looked.

Then in a moment of weakness,
The devil worked his way in.
He started to offer relief for my pain.
His goal: to get me to sin.

He must have been so happy
When I gave in to his lies.
Just because I was now a Christian
Didn't mean that I was wise.

The Son came shining through the clouds
That covered my life for so long.
As I felt the warmth of His brilliant light,
My weak soul somehow became strong.

As I sat and thought in the warmth of His love,
This beautiful truth filled my mind:
Through all the days I thought He was gone,
He was right here with me all the time.

I was just beginning to grow and learn
Why He loved me so much.
He lovingly stayed by my side,
And He touched me with His healing touch.

My life has never been the same
Since I surrendered my life to His will.
And in spite of the times I disobey Him,
He loves me and touches me still.

God's Man

God sends His man for the hour
To search for the sheep who are lost.
To unashamedly preach His Word
To win them at any cost.

Some thirteen years ago now,
God sent His man our way
To proclaim His wonderful truth.
To show forth the light of day.

It was to this place where God called you.
You stood on that beautiful day
And showed me through God's Holy Word,
Jesus, the Light, the Truth, the Way.

Because of that day in my life,
My blinded eyes can now see.
My heart's door I opened to Jesus,
And He now owns the key.

I'm eternally thankful to you, God's man,
For doing what God called you to do.
May He shower His blessings on you.
May His anointing fall fresh and anew.

Jesus Is the Answer

Almost eight years ago now,
I let Jesus into my heart.
I left behind all my failures,
And on a new life I did start.

Starting out as a new babe in Christ,
I fell prey to the devil's sly lies.
Before I realized, he had taken my joy
And had cunningly blinded my eyes.

Losing hope, I turned to the world
For an answer to my sorrow and woe.
The world had all the answers it seemed.
I jumped in and started downward to go.

The drugs they gave me seemed to help.
I saw things in a new way.
But unaware I was plunging
Deeper in despair day by day.

I soon lost the will to live.
Life was now such a chore.
I became a slave to the answer.
Nothing had meaning anymore.

But in my despair, Jesus came.
He broke the chains that had me bound.
As I looked into His beautiful face,
I knew the true answer I'd found.

Since then, He has been the answer.
All problems I lay at His feet.
With the assurance that He is in charge,
Each new day I cheerfully meet.

I still have a long way to go.
A lot of growing to do.
But now that I have the answer,
I'm sure I'll make it through.

Today with Jesus

Yesterday is gone,
And tomorrow is far away.
We must see how much Jesus can
Accomplish through us today.

It's really not very important
What we've done in days gone by.
We must concentrate on today.
And again, self must die.

We must yield ourselves to God.
And time in our busy day find
To fall on our faces before Him,
And cry out for lost mankind.

We must live our lives so that others
Around us can look and see
That the Savior who died for us all
Is *alive* and living in you and me.

We must use every opportunity
To witness to those who are lost.
To tell those in debt to sin
That Jesus has paid the cost.

Nothing is too much to ask.
Nothing is too much to give
For the One who saved us from death
That we might abundantly live.

Jesus called us to labor
For the harvest, indeed, is great.
He commanded us to go forth and preach.
Now's the time! We mustn't wait.

We mustn't be concerned with earthly wealth
But take care of the business at hand.
For the treasures we store up in heaven
Are the only ones that will stand.

We must make every minute count
For how swiftly the time does pass.
And we're not promised any tomorrows,
And today may be our last.

The Good Shepherd

The Good Shepherd looked over His flock
On that beautiful, sunny day
To see if all of His sheep were still there
Or if any had wandered away.

Most were gathered together
To call out unto Him.
But a few had wondered so far away,
Their view had become very dim.

He looked at the faithful before Him.
He could see that they were all right.
So He left them to go find the strays
Who were wandering alone in the night.

I know because I was one of the strays
Who was wandering and somehow lost sight
Of the One who had taken my darkness away
And replaced it with glorious light.

But one day I awoke in confusion,
Looked around, and realized I was lost.
Somehow I had to find my way back to the fold,
Whatever might be the cost.

As I desperately wandered in the darkness
Miserable, afraid, and alone,
The light shone through with all His brilliance
And illumined the path that led home.

He set my feet on the path.
He reached out and took my hand.
He said, "Come follow Me through all eternity,
And I'll take you to the Promised Land."

The Good Shepherd gave His life for the sheep.
Nothing was too much to give.
He desired that not any of His sheep would perish
But that they all might abundantly live.

To a stranger, they may all look alike.
But He knows each one by name.
He knows all there is to know about them.
And He loves us all just the same.

The Sweater

I sat down to knit a sweater
With needles and four kinds of yarn.
As I started, I asked Jesus
What spiritual truth I could learn.

As I worked and mixed the colors,
The pattern started to appear.
The more and more I knitted,
The similarity became more clear.

Life is like a sweater,
With sorrows and joys intertwined.
And only when Jesus is the main color
Can we have peace of mind.

Without Him as the foundation,
The pattern becomes all confused.
The colors all run together.
The sweater cannot be used.

If we want to be a sweater
That Jesus can wear and fill,
We must accept Him as our Lord
And turn over to Him our will.

What kind of sweater are you?
Are you folded, lying on a shelf?
Or can Jesus wear you each day?
Today, won't you ask yourself?

CHAPTER 4

Sweet Communion

O my dove, that art in the clefts of the rock,
in the secret places of the stairs, let me see thy
countenance, let me hear thy voice; for sweet is
thy voice, and thy countenance is comely.

—Song of Solomon 2:14

The Messenger of God

My Jesus spoke to me today
Through a messenger He sent my way.
He told me He loved me, not to despair.
He said He would always care.

He told me He cared enough to be born
Into a world of mockery and scorn.
He told me He cared enough to die
And that I'd be with Him by and by.

He told me I must stay a little longer.
He told me I had to be stronger.
He said I had to accept His love
If I wanted to live with Him above.

He said I must my whole self give
If I ever wanted to learn to live.
He said through Him was the only way
To die and go to heaven someday.

He told me to always spread His Word
To try to reach those who never heard
That He loves them, about Calvary,
To try to help their eyes to see.

He told me my life would be a chore.
He said each day to love Him more.
To let others know what He means to me.
To help them to set their souls free.

A True Friend

One morning I awoke in sadness.
The clouds of doubt covered my mind.
As the day began, I decided
To see if one friend I could find.

As I arose and looked into the mirror
At the stranger who stared back at me,
I thought how much I hated her,
And no hope for my search could I see.

If I had no love for this person
Whom I saw day in and day out,
Could anyone possibly love her?
I had a serious doubt.

Then from somewhere I heard a voice
That said, "Mary, I love you.
I know exactly how you feel.
Sometimes on earth I felt that way too.

"I know right now it seems hard
To find one friend you can depend on.
But I bore that for you, so when this time came,
I'd be here for you to lean on.

"I gave My life because I love you.
So that we could be together in the end.
But for the time you have left on earth,
I'd like to be called your friend."

So what seemed so hopeless in the beginning,
The search that had made me sad,
Just opened my eyes so I could see
The dearest friend I've ever had.

His Footprints

I awoke early one morning
And wondered what was happening to me.
As I looked on the floor beside the bed,
There, footprints I could clearly see.

I wondered, *Who has been here?*
Someone was here and has gone.
And I set out to follow the footprints
In the light of the early dawn.

I was taken away in the spirit.
On clouds, I did ride through the skies.
I found myself standing in heaven
And could hardly believe my eyes.

Before me there sat a beautiful throne.
I knew it belonged to the King.
The footprints led to the throne.
Then they led away again.

I was brought back to earth by an angel.
I saw a bright star in the flight.
This must be the star that shone brightly
On that first Christmas night.

The footprints led to a stable
Filled with animals and hay and things.
In the back was a crude little manger
That had held the King of Kings.

I followed the footprints to a garden.
I could tell many years had passed.
Someone had prayed in this garden,
A prayer that would always last.

The footprints left the garden.
I followed them up a hill.
A cross stood where Jesus gave His life
In accordance with the Father's will.

To our Lord's grave I followed the footprints.
I felt despair, defeat, and gloom.
But my heart rejoiced as I saw
The footprints led away from an empty tomb!

In excitement, I ran from the scene
I had thought was to be the end.
As I mounted a cloud, I was taken
Up to heaven again.

I stood before an empty throne.
I wondered, *But how can this be?*
I know I've come to the right place!
His footprints I clearly see!

In sadness, I sat on the bed,
The footprints still in front of me.
I looked toward heaven and cried,
"My Jesus, where can You be?"

But then I heard a voice answer,
"Child, I'm here to never depart.
I've been here all along.
I sit on the throne of your heart.

"I promised never to leave you,
To stay with you all the way.
I just set the footprints before you
For you to follow day by day.

"To show you wherever you go,
That I've already been there
To lighten the dark path ahead.
To show you how much I care.

"And never forget in the future
The search that you made today.
And remember, whenever you need Me,
I'm only a prayer away."

A Father's Love

When I, as a little child
Through the neighborhood did roam,
Suddenly, I'd hear my father's voice
Saying, "Child, it's time to come home."

No matter where I went,
Or how far away I'd go,
Above all the noise and bustle,
The sound of his voice I'd know.

With a gentle and loving sound,
He'd call me to his side.
And with a smile, he would greet me
With his arms opened wide.

My father has gone on before me.
I remember him oft with a tear.
And when I recall the love in his voice,
I wish that he were still here.

But I have a heavenly Father,
Whose love is beyond compare.
And He speaks to me in a loving voice
When I go to Him in prayer.

When sometimes like a child
I tend to wander away,
"It's time to come home, My child,"
I hear Him gently say.

When as I turn in response to His voice,
I'm filled with a peace inside.
And I see the loving smile on His face
As I run to His arms opened wide.

My Three Fathers

There is my heavenly Father,
Who blesses me beyond measure.
And His Son is preparing a place
Where I'm storing all my treasure.

He gave me an earthly father
To meet my physical needs.
To teach me right from wrong,
To plant eternal seeds.

Then He sent those who watered the seed
As I moved along life's way,
To bring me to the place
Where I was on that day.

When He sent my spiritual father
To introduce me to God's Son,
And as I yielded my life that day,
My soul, for the Lord, was won.

And I thank my heavenly Father
For the fathers He's given to me.
The one who taught me to walk,
And the one who taught me to see.

Jesus knows that I love my three fathers
More than mere words could ever say.
This message is sent to say thank you
For all you've done and still do each day.

The Change

I thought the sky had to be sunny
For it to be a beautiful day.
And today, though the clouds hide the sun,
It's beautiful anyway.

I look at myself; I don't understand
The change that has taken place.
Could it be the prayers of others,
Along with God's wonderful grace?

While trying to please others,
I lost my identity.
But as I stand back to take a clear look,
My true self I finally see.

The emotions that I so long suppressed
I finally allow to show through.
The me that I show to myself
Is no longer different from the me I show you.

It's such a relief to remove the mask
I've worn for so many years.
The person that you now see
Is capable of a smile or tears.

Dear Lord, help me live and grow each day.
Don't allow me to stand still.
Help me to love the person I've found,
And keep me safe in Your will.

Don't ever allow me to hide behind
A mask of fantasy.
But Lord, help me in every situation
To be no one but *me*.

Help me, Lord, to show others,
The love that You've shown me.
And somehow help the person I've found
To become more and more like Thee.

CHAPTER 5

Praise

Let every thing that hath breath praise the Lord. Praise ye the Lord.

—Psalm 150:6

But thou art holy, o thou that inhabitest the praises of Israel.

—Psalm 22:3

Prayer of Praise

Let everything that hath breath praise the Lord. (Psalm 150:6)

I praise You, Jesus. I love You, Lord.
For You gave me life when I didn't want to live.
You gave me hope when there was no hope left.
You loved me when I didn't even love myself.
I don't understand it, but in faith, I believe it.
Through faith, I accept it.
You are the light that shines in the darkness.
You are the guide that directs my path.
You are the foundation upon which my life is built.
You are my God, my Savior, my Lord, my Master, my deliverer,
my healer, my strength.
My shield, my joy, my peace, my hope, my Creator, my bread,
my water, my life, my Shepherd,
My coming King, and yet You are my closest friend, my brother!
You never let me down; You're always here when I need You,
And oh, how I need You.
May I be what You would have me to be.
May I go where You would have me to go.
May I do the things that You would do.
May Your love so shine through me that others would look past
me and see You.
May I be an instrument used by You.
Out of dust You formed me; I am but dust, and to dust I shall return,
But my soul shall live forever, with You, hallelujah!
And I will praise Your name forever and ever.
Praise You, Jesus! Praise You, Lord!

More Praise

And we know that all things work together for good to them that love God, to them who are the called according to His purpose. (Romans 8:28)

I do love You, Lord, and I am called, called to be a believer, a child of the King, a messenger, a witness, a light, an example, a follower, a disciple, a new creation, a servant, a martyr to self, a true friend, a living sacrifice, a prayer warrior, a joint-heir with Jesus.

Hallelujah!

And because of the sureness of my calling, I am assured that no matter what I encounter in life must work together for my good according to Your divine plan and purpose for my life.

Thank You, Jesus, for loving me, for calling me, and for working all things together for my good.
My God, how great Thou art!

Hallelujah! Hallelujah!

My Nurse

When I awoke this morning
And saw my nurse was there,
It gave me peace within
Because I know she cares.

You see, God sent her my way
Because He knew my fears.
She laughs and shares my joys,
And at times, she dries my tears.

When I awoke this morning,
I whispered a silent prayer
To thank God for my nurse,
He sent because He cares.

The Unseen Forces

The community waited in darkness
For someone to show them the light.
The E. E. Ministry was started,
And the troops prepared for the fight.

The combat forces were eager
As they polished their swords and their shields.
For they saw the harvest was abundantly white
As they looked out across God's field.

Another troop was preparing.
And in fact, had already begun/
They may not be seen on the front lines,
But with their help, the battle is won.

They march not as the others, before men,
Proclaiming the truth through the Word.
But they march in solitude on their knees,
Where, by God alone, they are heard.

The Master, in love and mercy,
Assigned an important task to each.
And as we march together hand in hand,
The lost, in His name, we can reach.

Tonight we give special thanks
For the forces no one ever sees.
The prayer partners of the E. E.,
The forces that march on their knees.

Note: E. E. stands for Evangelism Explosion, a training program
for Christians to become more effective witnesses for Christ.

CHAPTER 6

Verses for Special Occasions

Wherefore comfort yourselves together, and edify one another, even as also ye do.

—1 Thessalonians 5:11

Holidays

The days seem to come and go
With the swiftness of the wind.
A new year starts, and before we turn around,
We find that it's time for it to end.

There are some successes and some joys
As we seek to fulfill our dreams.
But there are also trials and troubles
Along the way; sometimes too many, it seems.

As we prepare for the holidays,
Our thoughts turn to family and friends.
We plan our schedules to fit in some time
So a few minutes with our loved ones we can spend.

The holidays pass by quickly,
In the blink of an eye.
We take it for granted, they'll be here next year.
We never even think they may die.

We all have a number of days here on earth.
No one knows what number or why.
Or how much pain and suffering we must bear
Before we're freed from this body and head for the sky.

As you celebrate this holiday,
This happy time of the year,
Take time to smell the roses.
Enjoy each moment with those you hold dear.

And when the holidays are over,
Remember how swiftly time flies.
Enjoy your loved ones all year long.
Don't let this precious time pass by.

Make every moment last as long as it will.
Savor it's sweetness, and place it in your heart.
Then no matter what life might put in your way,
The memories of the special times never have to part.

Try Something New

The brilliant colors of fall have passed.
There is a briskness in the air.
And even though Thanksgiving's not here yet,
Preparations for Christmas are everywhere.

The numerous ads show sale after sale.
Those gifts have got to be bought.
And we hurry and scurry to get it all done
Without really giving much thought.

What is this season really all about?
What's the true reason for this time of year?
And we work and worry until we're so tired
We can't relax and enjoy it while it's here.

Imagine a year when we didn't have a list.
And we didn't ponder about what to get whom.
And we didn't spend days cooking food we don't need.
We decided to do something new.

We decided to take time spent on gifts
To sit down and talk to each other.
To give something that can't be bought in stores,
Memories of time spent enjoying one another.

God showed us the way that first Christmas Day.
He gave us the greatest gift of all.
He wasn't bought, wrapped, or put under a tree.
He was alive, lying in a manger, innocent and small.

He gave us one gift for the whole world—
A part of Himself, His Son.
He's always there to help lighten our burden.
His fellowship gives peace when the day is done.

What if instead of buying gifts
We gave each other what God gave to us?
Sharing our love, spending time together,
Sprinkling every day with a little Christmas!

Thanksgiving

Thanksgiving is the time of year
When we thank God for His blessing.
And families gather from far and near
For the traditional turkey and dressing.

Somehow we wait until this time of year
To get in touch with those we love.
To tell them how much they mean to us
And give thanks to our Father above.

What a shame only one day a year
Is set aside for this reason.
The Bible says, "In all things give thanks,"
Every day, every month, every season.

So what is the purpose of this rhyme?
The reason: For you to see very clearly.
I want to remind you at this special time
That I love each one of you dearly.

Preparing for Christmas

As we prepare to celebrate
The birthday of our King—
Who was the most precious gift of all time—
Gifts to our loved ones we bring.

The love that was born on that first Christmas Day
We feel in us and around us today.
We try to express it and share it with others
As we hustle and bustle on our way.

This poem and our hearts are filled with this love,
And we send it to you with good cheer.
May you and yours have a blessed Christmas,
And may you feel our love all year.

The Night the Light Was Born

The world awaited in darkness
To behold the heavenly light.
The light, who was born in a stable
And laid in a manger that night.

Angels filled the heavens
To announce His holy birth.
The Savior of all mankind
Had come from heaven to earth.

Shepherds left their flocks
To behold the heavenly sight.
It was the King of Kings
They met that holy night.

Jesus left His throne of glory
To fulfill salvation's plan.
It was His love that caused Him
To come, willing to die for man.

It's because of that wonderful love
We celebrate this time of year.
We gather together with family and friends,
And our hearts are filled with cheer.

This poem is written to share this love
With those who are dearest to us.
May God shower you with countless blessings
As we worship Him this glorious Christmas!

Noel

N is for the *night* that Jesus turns to day.

O is for the fact that He is the *only* way.

E is for the *everlasting* life as Christians we live.

L is for the *love* He was born and died to give.

Christmas

C is for the *cry* that came forth from lost mankind.
H is for the *hope* that brings peace to the troubled mind.
R is for the *redeemer* sent from heaven above.
I is for *Israel* to whom He showed His love.
S is for the *salvation* He provided for all who believe.
T is for the *treasure,* which with Him, we will receive.
M is for the *mercy,* though undeserved, He shows you and me.
A is for the *angels* who protect us, even though we can't see.
S is for the *suffering* He lovingly faced for all of us.

So we should rejoice and sing praises to Him on this glorious day
called Christmas!

The Greatest Gift of All

One night thousands of years ago,
In a stable unnoticed by most,
The Savior of mankind was born
And was greeted by a heavenly Host.

Some shepherds who were watching their sheep,
By angels were told of His birth.
And they went to Bethlehem to see
That the Son of God had come to earth.

A huge star in the heavens marked the place.
And some wise men followed it to see
If this was the Messiah, who had been prophesied,
Coming to save you and me.

They bowed down in His presence,
Even though they themselves were kings.
They offered gifts of gold, frankincense, and myrrh
As they realized this was the King of Kings.

I am so thankful for that night,
When Jesus left heaven and came to earth,
So that we who were dead in our sins
Might accept Him and experience new birth.

Because He grew up and took all our sin
And defeated death by going to Calvary,
All who accept Him can have abundant life
And everlasting life with Him in eternity.

The Gift of Love

In a stable years ago,
Our Savior came to earth.
And Christmas came into being
To celebrate His glorious birth.

The King came down from heaven above
To bring salvation, peace, and joy.
The greatest gift of love ever given
Was wrapped up in this tiny baby boy.

The angels spread the joyous news
To shepherds at work in the field.
They left their flocks to go and see
The Savior of man as the Father willed.

Many years have come and gone.
The story has been rearranged
As we hurry about in our stress-filled lives,
Trying to gain all that can be gained.

We think silently about how much money
Someone is spending on our gift this year.
Of course, so we'll know what to spend on theirs.
Not pleasing them becomes our biggest fear.

Where is the real Spirit of Christmas
That gives peace, hope, joy, and love?
Christmas isn't about how much we receive,
But how much love was given freely from above.

And we don't even have to wait for Christmas.
That same love in abundance is ours every day.
But we must reach out and accept it.
For to receive it, that is the only way.

What would you do this Christmas morn
If your best friend came to your door,
Bearing no visible gift in their hand
But said, "You must invite me in to receive more."

Would you be hurt and disappointed,
Thinking they no longer care?
Or would you continue to thank God for a friend
As you silently utter a prayer?

Then they say, "You're so special to me,
I wanted to give you something that would never depart.
So I decided to give you the most precious gift,
The love I feel for you that has become a part of my heart."

Easter

E is for the *everlasting* life He bought for you and me.

A is for the *agony* He faced in Gethsemane.

S is for the *shame* He bore that was really yours and mine.

T is for the *tree* on which He died for all mankind.

E is for the *empty* tomb that left His disciples forlorn.

R is for the *resurrection* that took place that first Easter morn!

At last He had fulfilled the purpose for which He was born! Hallelujah!

He Is Alive!

The disciples huddled together in fear,
On this horrible night filled with gloom,
As they hid from the outside world
Locked in that small upper room.

Were they going to be next?
Were they going to die?
This wasn't the plan,
And they all questioned, "Why?"

Where was the kingdom
That Jesus came to build?
They could not understand
As with grief their hearts were filled.

In the early dawn, as the sun rose
At the beginning of the third day,
The women came to anoint His body.
But the stone was rolled away.

The tomb where they had laid Him
Now was empty and bare.
As they entered, they saw His body was gone.
Had it been taken? By whom and to where?

They were frightened by the presence of angels
Who assured them not to fear.
"We know you've come to seek Jesus,
But He is risen! He is not here!"

He had fulfilled what He had told them.
The words they could not understand.
He had become the one and only sacrifice
Who could forever bring about the redemption of man.

So on this glorious Easter morning,
Sing praises to His holy Name!
For He alone is worthy,
The Lamb, who for us, was slain.

Hallelujah! He is alive!

Friend

F is for the *faithfulness* You've shown in standing by me.

R is for the many *reminders* of Your love I see.

I is for the *incredible* one You are in accomplishing all that You do.

E is for the *everlasting* love I have for You.

N is for the joyous fact that our friendship will *never* end.

D is for the *day*; I'm so thankful for that day You became my friend.

CHAPTER 7

Family Poems

For this cause I bow my knees unto the Father of our Lord Jesus Christ of whom the whole family in earth and heaven is named, that He would grant you, according to His riches in glory, to be strengthened with might by His Spirit in the inner man;

That Christ may dwell in your hearts by faith; that ye, being rooted and grounded in love, may be able to comprehend with all the saints what is the breadth, and length, and depth, and height; and to know the love of Christ, which passeth knowledge, that ye might be filled with all the fullness of God.

—Ephesians 3:14–19

To Jim

Some thirty-five years ago now,
You first came into my life.
It never entered my mind at the time
That we'd ever be husband and wife.

But as time passed and love took hold,
We found ourselves saying, "I do."
Blinded by love, we never realized
How much trouble two words could get you into.

The years have not been easy.
Sometimes very rough was the way.
We never understood a lot of things,
But we have some of the answers today.

The last year has been especially hard,
Not knowing which way to go at times.
We both had to reevaluate everything,
And it's enough to blow our minds.

I'm not really sure where we are right now.
I'm not sure about our tomorrows.
I don't think either of us know right now
If we can forget and overcome all the sorrows.

It's just like starting over again.
We're just getting to know each other.
We've still got a lot of things to work out,
A lot of ground to cover.

Because of You

Thanks for always being there.
Whether near or far, even when we're apart,
I always know you care
'Cause I feel it in my heart.

Thanks for always knowing when I need
A smile, a word, or a hug.
For knowing sometimes I need to be alone,
And at those times, not being a bug.

Thanks for always knowing that there are
Also times I need you by my side
To give me a reason to face tomorrow
As this life's waves ebb and tide.

Thanks for all the little things you do
That you might think I'm not aware.
Talking, listening, sharing, or just being there.
All these special things say, "I care."

Thanks for letting me know in this chaotic world
There's someone who thinks and feels as I do.
You make my life worth going on
Because I'm assured I'll always have you.

Punkin (Dianna)

On June 8, 1967, God sent our first baby girl.
As I looked at her sweet little face and counted her fingers and toes,
I realized that I was a mother.
But how to do that, only God knows.

As I held her in my arms,
Love flowed over my heart.
Her dad smiled from ear to ear
As the three of us on our new life did start.

She couldn't wait till her daddy came home from work.
Out the door to play they did go.
She crawled and walked, made sounds and talked.
All too fast did the time go.

We moved when she was two.
She had her own room and a big yard in which to play.
We went back to check if we got everything.
Off came her coat, and she was ready to stay.

As she became a young lady,
Her beauty was beyond compare.
She had to dress just so,
And she took forever to fix her hair.

She had several good friends.
Together, with each, she could play.
But put all three together,
And it became another D-Day!

She didn't like school at all,
Except as a place to see her friends.
But she would go every day,
So she wouldn't have to take exams at year's end.

She worked every day at the bank.
I realized that she was truly grown.
Then one day she became a mother
With a husband and a baby all her own.

I knew that she would always be first,
Our sweet baby like no other.
As I look back, I realize that because of her,
I first became a mother.

Mark's Holiday

The banks and schools are closed today.
They won't deliver the mail.
They say it's because of some celebrity.
But we would never tell.

If you would like to make people think
They did it all for you.
They're not the only one who can claim today
Because it's your birthday too.

So if anybody should ask you
Why you're off today,
Just smile at them and reply,
"It's Mark Stancil's holiday."

So we officially declare
It's Mark Stancil's birthday holiday.
And we hope that today and all year
Only good things come your way.

And don't ever let anyone tell you
That you're not as important as "he."
And you can tell your children,
"One year they made a holiday for me."

The Wildman (Brandon)

He calls himself the "Wildman,"
And I have to partially agree.
At ten, he's certainly not a man,
But the wild part I can plainly see.

His energy never ceases.
His mouth is seldom quiet.
He hates to take a bath
Or to go to bed at night.

He loves to wrestle and play with his dad.
He never knows when to quit.
He thinks he can do anything.
When challenged, he doesn't hesitate a bit.

He likes to play ball and ride his bike,
Play his Sega, go skating, and swim.
He likes to go to church and play with the kids next door.
And watching TV is an everyday thing for him.

He is really very smart.
He tries to make you think he is mum.
He thinks that gives him an excuse to goof off.
And he drives me out of my mind sucking his thumb.

He has to be reminded of everything,
Or he would forget his head.
He hates to clean up his room
And has to be threatened to make up his bed.

He has to be told to keep his knees off the couch
And to slow down and chew when he eats.
Not to wear shorts in the wintertime
And that his homework needs to be neat.

He's very particular about his hair
And has to "water it" every day.
He says it has to look just right,
But to mess it up there's no way.

He already has a girlfriend
That he writes notes and gives presents to.
But I guess when you stop and think of all these things,
It's pretty typical of what most ten-year-old boys do.

I guess they are all kind of wild
Little boys when they're ten.
And we hope that they outgrow it all
Before they become men.

My Precious Rose (Patti)

It was a day in late summer 1974,
A priceless gift came from above.
She was a tiny, fragile rose,
So beautiful, so easy to love.

This beautiful, tiny, fragile rose
Required much care from the start.
So I placed her safely where she would stay warm.
I sheltered her in the center of my heart.

I couldn't understand why our Father above
Would bless me with such a special gem.
He knew I certainly didn't have a green thumb,
So on Him, I would have to depend.

As the winter came with its treacherous winds,
I fought desperately to help my rose survive.
The winter was so cold and so long.
Spring finally came; my rose was barely alive.

Through many winters we rode the storms,
Not understanding the reason why
We were faced with so many storms,
While so many others the storms would pass by.

Then one day I looked and realized
That while fighting the winter storms all,
My beautiful, tiny, fragile rose
Had grown very strong and tall.

I stood back and looked, almost in fear,
To assess the damage I knew must be there.
To my surprise, as she grew strong and tall,
Her beauty had a radiant glow; I couldn't help but stare.

Before my eyes, my tiny, fragile rose
Had weathered the storms' strong winds and tide.
And instead of a weak, withered, fading rose,
A rose of the rarest beauty was standing strong and tall on the
other side.

Then, with a tear in my eye but a smile on my lips,
I realized my priceless gift sent from above
No longer needed my constant shelter and care
But would forever remain in my heart, held close by my love.

Happy Father's Day

I started out on this:
Your special day
To try to show my love
In some small way.

I sat down and wondered,
What could I do
To show you how much
I love you?

I could have spent a lot of money
For something oh, so nice.
I could have baked a rich dessert
Filled with sugar and spice.

I chose to spend a little time
And make you something else.
I somehow thought it might mean more
If I gave part of myself.

I sat down to write on paper
Just how I feel within.
And as I sit here thinking,
I don't know where to begin.

I'd like to thank you for all
The things you say and do.
And ask you always to remember
How much I love you.

I think if I searched
The whole world through,
I'd never find another
Dad as wonderful as you.

Happy Birthday, Mom

I look at the hair that once was dark
But now is white with years.
I look at the smiling eyes
That many times were filled with tears.

I read in the lines upon your face
The troubles you have known.
And I see in the sweetness of your smile
The love you have always shown.

I look at the hands, now swollen with pain,
That have performed many a chore.
They've washed and scrubbed and cooked and sewed.
All these, and so many more.

But as I look in this face of love,
I see the beauty of no other.
And I thank God every day that He
Chose you to be my mother.

Happy Anniversary!

Moms and Dads are special.
So special in so many ways.
That's why we ought to remember them
On all their special days.

On this day so many years ago,
You both said, "I do."
You promised to love, honor, and obey
Through the good and the bad too.

I imagine that there has been plenty of both
Through so many years.
I know there were times filled with laughter and smiles.
But there was also time for tears.

You both mean so much to us all.
We can never truly express our love.
I rejoice when I think we've been a family down here,
And we'll be part of God's family above.

And I'm sure as you look back over the years,
Your hearts are filled with glee
As you think of the year 1947,
When you were blessed to have me!

Happy Valentine's Day

Love is that special gift
That comes only from above.
For the Word in describing God
Tells us He is love.

On this Valentine's Day
I set out seeking to find
The words I could use to express
What's really on my mind.

Optional Last Verses:

When I think of the word *love*,
I always think of you.
For if I searched the whole world over,
I'd never find anyone else like you.

Sweetheart or Mate:

When I think of the word *love*,
My thoughts all turn to you.
For if I searched the whole world over,
I'd never find a sweetheart like you.

or

Through the years I've known you,
I've grown to love you more and more.
And on this special day for lovers,
I love you more than ever before.

Parents

When I think of the word *love,*
My thoughts all turn to you.
For no other parents I know
Give of themselves as you do.

or

And so, on this special day,
We wanted to let you know
How special you are to us.
Our love somehow to show.

Happy Valentine's Day, Sweetheart

All thoughts are turned to sweethearts
Every Valentine's Day.
And we try to express our love
In some little, thoughtful way.

Some sixteen years ago now,
You first entered my life.
I had no idea then
That I would ever be your wife.

But as the days passed by,
I soon came to discover
I wanted you forever to be
My husband and my lover.

And according to God's plan,
We vowed each other to love
Through the good times and the bad
Til we are with Him above.

God has called us as one
To share His love with the lost,
The love He showed you and me
When He paid the awful cost.

And as we think of sweethearts,
And our thoughts are turned to love,
Let us never forget the perfect love
God sent us from above.

And it thrills me on this Valentine's Day
To say, "I love you sweetheart."
And though we won't always be husband and wife,
We will never have to part.

CHAPTER 8

Songs

Speaking to yourselves in psalms and hymns and spiritual songs, singing and making melody in your heart to the Lord.

—Ephesians 5:19

Seek Ye First

Chorus
Seek ye first the kingdom of God.
Seek ye first His righteousness.
Take no thought what you eat, drink, and wear
For all these things shall be given you.

Verse 1
Have you ever watched the fowls of the air?
For they sow not neither do they reap.
For the Father feeds them and they worry not.
Unlike man, they never lose any sleep.

Chorus

Verse 2
Consider the lilies of the field.
They toil not, neither do they spin.
If God clothes them in glory,
Do you think He forgets about men?

Chorus

Verse 3
So take ye no thought for tomorrow,
Or the problems it may bring,
For our Lord, who knows all,
Is still the Kings of Kings.

Chorus

That Day

Chorus
The darkness covered the land.
The veil of the temple was rent in two.
The earth did quake, but love flowed free.
That day, the Savior died for me and you.

Verse 1
I went through life searching to fill the void within,
For something to give joy and peace and take away my sin.
While seeking an answer, God's Word, I found along the way.
As I turned the page and read the words, I learned about that day.

Chorus

Verse 2
The Son of God hung on a cross.
The sins of the world He bore.
There never was a day before or since like that day,
The day the darkness came that light may shine forevermore!

Chorus

Verse 3
That day I met the Savior, who gave His life for me.
I walked that lonely road and knelt at Calvary.
But no longer would I be alone as I walked on life's way.
Praise God! Thank You, Jesus, for what You did that day.

Chorus

Only One Way

Verse 1
Jesus tells us in the Word, that there are two ways.
One is broad and wide, the other narrow and straight.
He said many will go the broad and wide way,
But few will enter in the narrow gate.

Verse 2
The Bible says there is a way that seems right to man,
But the wages of that way is death.
Jesus said, "I am the way," and if we ask Him,
He will breathe into us everlasting breath.

Chorus
Only one way—the way, the truth, the life.
Only one way of salvation for us.
We may try all the ways the world can offer,
But there's only one way; His name is Jesus.

Verse 3
God, in His love and mercy, gave us a choice.
We are free to choose either way.
My friend, Jesus really loves you,
And He waits with open arms for you today.

Chorus

Jesus Is My Shelter

Chorus
Jesus is my shelter amid the storm.
He keeps me safe in this world of sin and strife.
The storms of fear and doubt would overtake me,
But in my shelter, I find peace and life.

Verse 1
I started down the road of life in victory,
Not expecting any storms to come my way.
Never realized that when you follow Jesus,
There is always a price you have to pay.

Chorus

Verse 2
Jesus never said it would be easy,
But He promises us shelter from the storm.
Weeping may endure for a night,
But praise God, joy cometh in the morn.

Chorus

Love One Another

Chorus
Love one another as I have loved you.
Love one another; this I command you to do.
Love one another, so others may look and see.
You are my disciples 'cause you love one another in me.

Verse 1
Jesus had met with His disciples
To break the final bread,
To give them a new commandment,
To prepare them for what lay ahead.

Chorus

Verse 2
He took a towel; He girded Himself.
He washed the disciples' feet.
They gathered around the table,
Their last meal together to eat.

Chorus

Verse 3
Jesus said that one would betray Him.
Each one questioned, "Is it I?"
When Jesus told Judas, "Do it quickly,"
He departed, and no one questioned why.

Chorus

Verse 4
And when he had gone out,
Jesus began to share what to do.
He said, "Where I go you cannot come,
So now this I say to you."

Chorus

Printed in the United States
by Baker & Taylor Publisher Services